# COOL SHORT-HAIRED CATS

Written by Eliza Jeffery    Illustrated by Marina Halak

Copyright © 2024 Hungry Tomato Ltd

First published in 2024 by Hungry Tomato Ltd
F15, Old Bakery Studios, Blewetts Wharf, Malpas Road, Truro, Cornwall,
TR1 1QH, UK.

No part of this publication may be reproduced, stored in a retrieval system, or transmitted in any form or by any means, electronic, mechanical, photocopying, recording, or otherwise, without prior written permission of the copyright owner.

A CIP catalogue record for this book is available from the British Library.

ISBN 9781835693445

Printed in China

Discover more at
www.hungrytomato.com

# CONTENTS

| | |
|---|---|
| The World of Cats | 4 |
| Keeping Clean and Healthy | 6 |
| Cool Cat Features | 8 |
| Cool Short-haired Cats | 10 |
| Curious and Active | 11 |
| Dark and Mysterious | 12 |
| Wild Look-alikes | 14 |
| Easy To Spot | 16 |
| Stand Out From the Crowd | 18 |
| Around the World | 20 |
| Cool Cat Facts | 22 |
| Cat Communication | 24 |
| Name That Cat | 26 |
| What's That Cat? | 28 |
| Glossary | 30 |
| Index | 31 |

Words in **BOLD** can be found in the glossary.

# THE WORLD OF CATS

Get ready to explore the wonderful world of cats! From the rare, green-eyed Havana to the bright, blue-eyed snowshoe, there are so many different types of cool cats to discover.

## WHAT IS A SPECIES?

A species is a group of living things, like animals or plants, that share **unique** characteristics. For example, leopards and **domestic** cats are two different species. Around 40 species of cats exist, which can then be split into different breeds.

## WHAT IS A BREED?

A breed is a small group of animals within a species that all share the same (or very similar) appearance and characteristics, making them easy to identify. There are lots of different breeds, and they can vary wildly in size, shape, personality, and hairiness.

Not all cats belong to a specific breed. Some cats are a mixture of lots of different breeds. They can make fantastic and unique pets, and can often be found looking for a loving home at rescue or **rehoming shelters**.

This breed looks a bit like a lion, but is actually domestic!

## WHERE DO CATS COME FROM?

All cats are **descendants** of the African wildcat, a species believed to have emerged 12 million years ago! This cat is still around today, alongside many other types of wild cat. There are plenty of new species that have been domesticated by humans too – these are the types of cats that we keep as pets!

Some cats can be cheeky and mischievous!

## GETTING A CAT?

Maybe you already have a cat in your family, or maybe you'd like to in the future. Owning a cat can be fun and rewarding, but it's also a big responsibility! Some cats need a lot of grooming, care and attention. Before buying or adopting a cat, you should always carefully research their breed and think about whether you are able to give them everything they need to be happy.

# KEEPING CLEAN AND HEALTHY

When it comes to taking care of a cat, there is a lot to consider! Some cats need a lot more looking after than others. Here are a few things to think about when you are looking into what your cat needs to be happy and healthy.

## GROOMING

Grooming is a very important part of owning a cat. Cats naturally clean themselves, often spending many hours a day licking their fur clean. Despite doing a lot of the hard work themselves, cats still need some help from their owners!

Short-haired cats don't need as much grooming as long-haired cats, but they do need a brush at least once a week to stop their fur from **matting**. They also need to be checked for fleas and ticks regularly.

You will often see your cat cleaning themselves in all sorts of positions!

## BATHING

It is important for cats to be given a bath once every 4-6 weeks to make sure they stay clean. Long-haired cats need baths more regularly, but it's still important for short-haired cats, too!

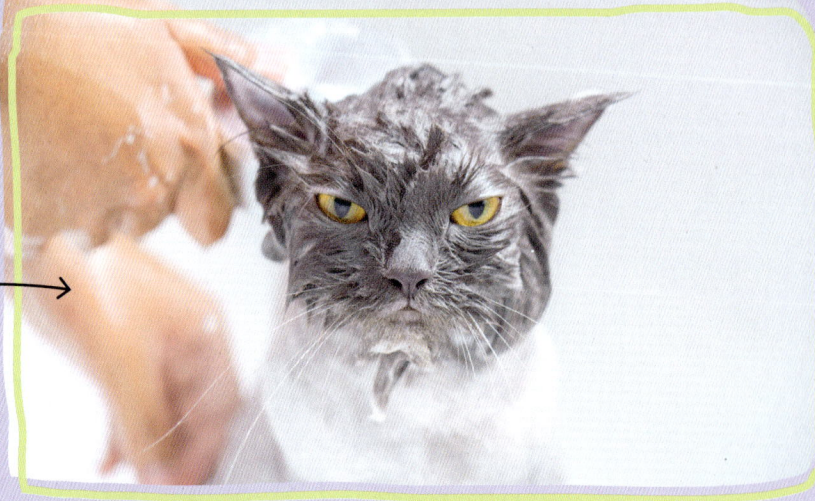

Cats don't usually enjoy being in water, so you will need to be patient when giving your cat a bath.

Getting your cat into a good bathing routine from an early age is important, and will help them stay more relaxed during bath time as they grow.

# CLEANING

Cats know how to keep themselves clean, but they need some help from their owners too! This includes checking their ears, brushing their teeth, cleaning their eyes and nose, and clipping their nails. Once again, patience is key for taking care of your cat!

## EARS

It is important to check that your cat's ears are clean and free of **ear wax**. If you notice your cat's ears are blocked, use tissue or a cotton wool ball to gently remove any wax.

## EYES AND NOSE

A wet cotton wool ball can be used to clear away any **mucus** or stains found around a cat's eyes and nose.

## TEETH

Cats need to brush their teeth too! It is recommended that you should brush your cat's teeth three times a week. You can use special cat toothpaste to encourage your cat to help with brushing.

## NAILS

Cats are good at keeping their nails short by exercising and using scratch posts, but it is important to keep an eye on them. Long nails can curl into your cat's paws and cause them pain if they get too long.

# COOL CAT FEATURES

**Explore some of the features that make cats such fascinating creatures! From their sharp teeth to their protective paws, discover the impressive adaptations that help cats thrive in their environments.**

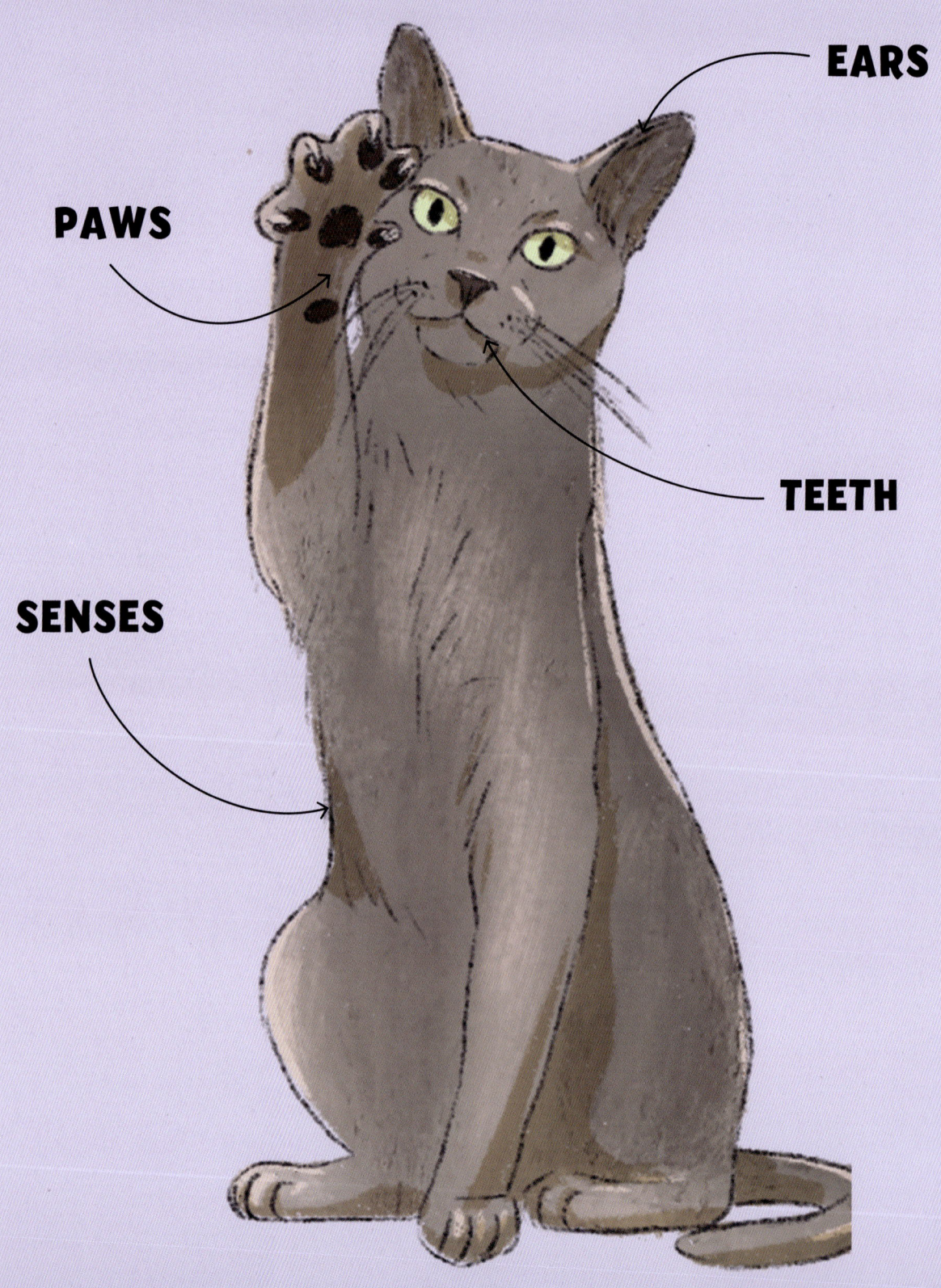

EARS

PAWS

TEETH

SENSES

## TEETH

All adult cats have 30 teeth. They have different teeth for different jobs. Some teeth are used for grooming, some for gripping onto objects, and some for chewing up their food!

## EARS

Cats have a special ability - they can move each ear separately! This means one ear can listen for sounds in one direction while the other ear listens somewhere else.

## PAWS

Cats have hairless pads on the bottom of their paws. This helps protect their paws from tough surfaces, as well as gives them as cushions to land safely on! Cats can have four or five toes on each paw.

## SENSES

Cats have impressive senses! They are born with a balancing system called the 'righting reflex', which, when a cat falls from a fence or tree, allows them to move in mid-air so they land the right way up!

# COOL SHORT-HAIRED CATS

Most cat species have developed short hair over time, including wild and domesticated breeds. This allows them to move and hunt easily, as well as keep them cool in warmer months.

The first cats to be domesticated are believed to have had a short coat of fur. When it comes to looking after domestic cats, the short-haired breeds are easy for owners to maintain, often only needing to be groomed once a week. Let's delve into the world of cool short-haired cats!

CURIOUS AND ACTIVE — 11

# Abyssinian

This wild-looking cat is believed to have descended from Ethiopia and been taken to the United Kingdom by soldiers in the 1860s. Abyssinians have a lean, muscular build and are extremely intelligent. They are playful creatures and make wonderful companions.

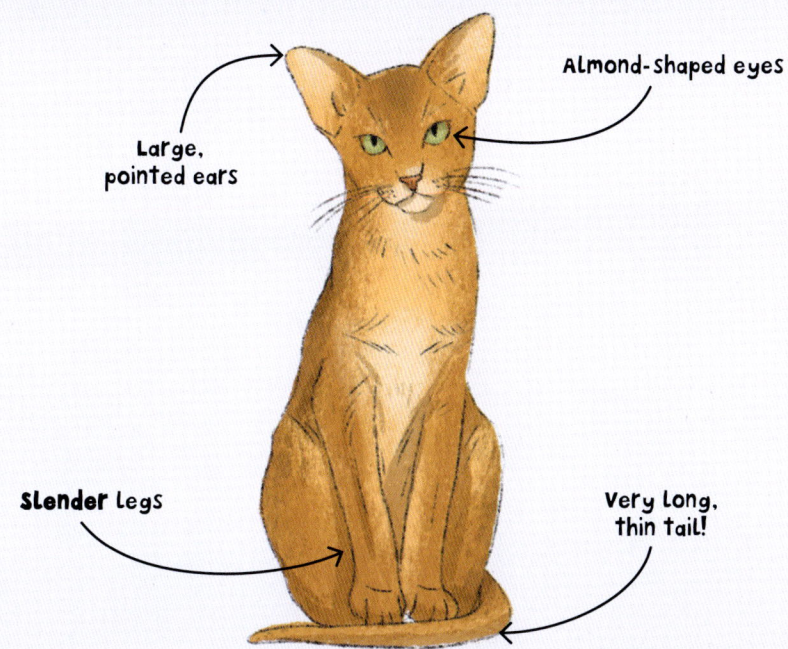

Large, pointed ears
Almond-shaped eyes
Slender legs
Very long, thin tail!

**ORIGIN:** Ethiopia
**COAT:** Short and glossy
**PERSONALITY:** Friendly and curious

GROOMING
AFFECTION
PLAYFULNESS

# Burmese

The Burmese is a lean and elegant cat with distinctive yellow eyes. They are great family pets that enjoy playing games and spending time with their owners. These pretty cats like lots of attention!

Large, yellow eyes!
Muscular body
Skinny legs
Soft fur all over

**ORIGIN:** Myanmar (formerly Burma)
**COAT:** Short and silky
**PERSONALITY:** Active and curious

GROOMING
AFFECTION
PLAYFULNESS

# COOL SHORT-HAIRED CATS

## Havana

The Havana is a rare breed, easy to spot thanks to their brown fur and bright, green eyes. They are very intelligent creatures that can be trained to play fetch! These felines are very sociable, so they don't like to be left alone for long periods of time.

Bright, green eyes!

Fur can be chocolatey-brown to almost black!

Thin, strong body

**ORIGIN:** USA
**COAT:** Short and smooth
**PERSONALITY:** Playful and gentle

GROOMING: 🐾🐾⚪⚪⚪
AFFECTION: 🐾🐾🐾🐾🐾
PLAYFULNESS: 🐾🐾🐾🐾⚪

## Korat

The Korat is considered a good luck charm in Thailand. This pretty feline's coat is always a silvery-blue, making its green eyes stand out! This sociable cat enjoys lots of interactive play and is very loving toward its owners.

Heart-shaped nose

They are believed to bring lots of good luck!

Muscular body

**ORIGIN:** Thailand
**COAT:** Short and shimmery
**PERSONALITY:** Affectionate and friendly

GROOMING: 🐾🐾⚪⚪⚪
AFFECTION: 🐾🐾🐾🐾⚪
PLAYFULNESS: 🐾🐾🐾🐾⚪

DARK AND MYSTERIOUS     13

# Chartreux

Chartreux are best known for their dark silver fur and round, golden eyes. They have a sturdy build, with a muscular body and strong legs. Chartreux are calm and quiet cats that appreciate lots of attention in the home. Even though these felines do enjoy playtime, they would much prefer to take a nap!

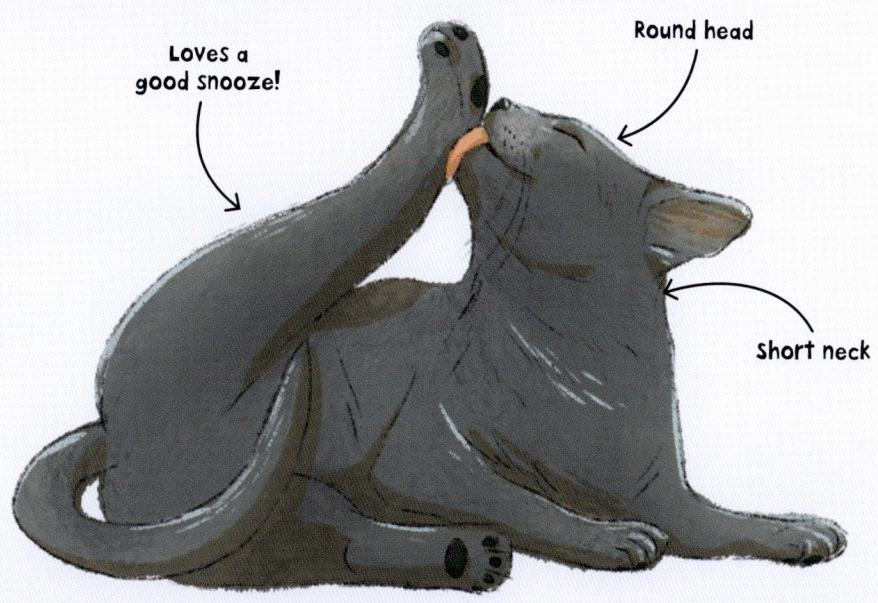

Loves a good snooze!
Round head
Short neck

**ORIGIN:** France
**COAT:** Thick and woolly
**PERSONALITY:** Quiet and curious

GROOMING
AFFECTION
PLAYFULNESS

# Bombay

This panther look-alike has a jet-black coat and gold, round eyes. These friendly felines are often found in warm, comfy spots around the house. The Bombay cat is very sociable and active with its owners.

Full face with rounded ears
Shiny coat
Strong back legs

**ORIGIN:** USA
**COAT:** Short and glossy
**PERSONALITY:** Mischievous and outgoing

GROOMING
AFFECTION
PLAYFULNESS

# COOL SHORT-HAIRED CATS

## Toyger

Nicknamed the "toy tiger", this breed of cat looks like a small version of a tiger! Despite looking like a wild cat, the toyger was bred to be sociable and friendly toward its owners and other household pets.

| | |
|---|---|
| **ORIGIN:** USA | |
| **COAT:** Short and dense | |
| **PERSONALITY:** Laid-back and friendly | |

GROOMING
AFFECTION
PLAYFULNESS

## Savannah

The Savannah is best known for its dog-like personality. Unlike many cats, this striking feline enjoys playing in water and loves to play fetch! This breed came from mixing a domestic cat with a wild serval, giving the Savannah its interesting coat pattern.

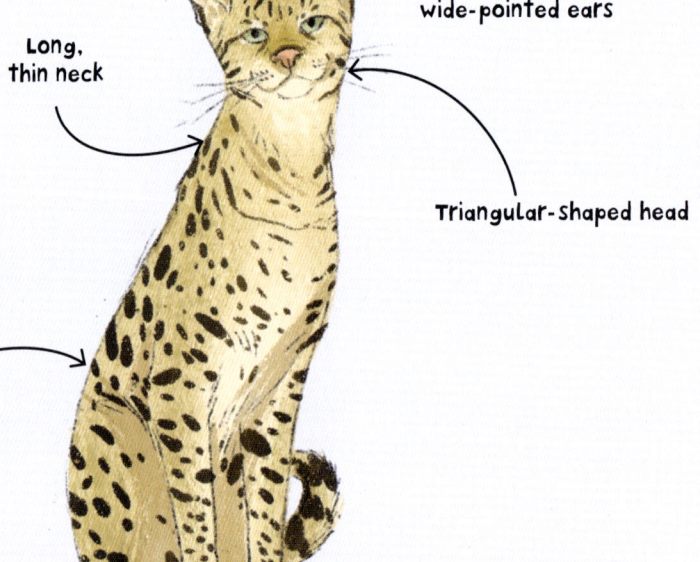

| | |
|---|---|
| **ORIGIN:** USA | |
| **COAT:** Short and dense | |
| **PERSONALITY:** Adventurous and loyal | |

GROOMING
AFFECTION
PLAYFULNESS

WILD LOOK-ALIKES    15

# Bengal

This striking feline is just as energetic and independent as its wild cat look-alike! Bengal cats have high energy levels, which means they are lots of fun to play with but can also be a handful for their owners!

- Tall ears
- Long, thin body
- Brown spots and stripes across the coat
- Strong, muscular legs

**ORIGIN:** USA
**COAT:** Short and soft
**PERSONALITY:** Active and curious

GROOMING 🐾🐾🐾🐾🐾
AFFECTION 🐾🐾🐾🐾🐾
PLAYFULNESS 🐾🐾🐾🐾🐾

# Ocicat

The ocicat has the same spotted tabby coat and distinctive, large eyes as an ocelot. The ocicat is athletic and intelligent, so it enjoys lots of attention from its owners. This wild-looking cat loves to explore and jump up high!

- Almond-shaped eyes
- Strong, muscular legs
- Oval-shaped paws

**ORIGIN:** USA
**COAT:** Thin and shiny
**PERSONALITY:** Energetic and curious

GROOMING 🐾🐾🐾🐾🐾
AFFECTION 🐾🐾🐾🐾🐾
PLAYFULNESS 🐾🐾🐾🐾🐾

# COOL SHORT-HAIRED CATS

# Snowshoe

The snowshoe is easy to spot by its bright blue eyes and distinctive mix of light and dark fur. Very playful and sociable, this sweet feline relies greatly on its owners, so it doesn't enjoy being left alone for too long!

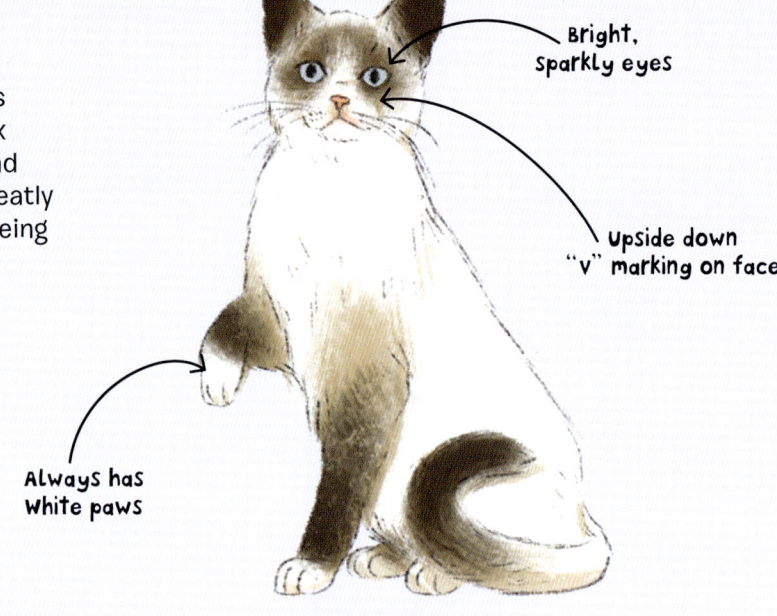

- Bright, sparkly eyes
- Upside down "v" marking on face
- Always has white paws

**ORIGIN:** USA
**COAT:** Short and thick
**PERSONALITY:** Sociable and affectionate

GROOMING 🐾🐾🐾
AFFECTION 🐾🐾🐾🐾🐾
PLAYFULNESS 🐾🐾🐾🐾🐾

- Long tail helps with balance
- Loves to play with toys, like balls and feather wands!

EASY TO SPOT 17

# Australian Mist

The Australian Mist was the first domestic cat to be bred in Australia. Its coat has a soft, shadowy appearance, which gives it its misty name. This friendly feline is a mix between an Abyssinian and Burmese cat (page 11).

Wide ears that tilt forward

Long, thick tail

can be cheeky and mischievous!

**ORIGIN:** Australia
**COAT:** Tough and glossy
**PERSONALITY:** Friendly and mellow

GROOMING
AFFECTION
PLAYFULNESS

# Sokoke

The Sokoke is a very rare breed of domesticated cat. These elegant felines make close family bonds and are known for communicating with their owners by meowing lots! They are considered one of the smartest cats in the world, and love to play.

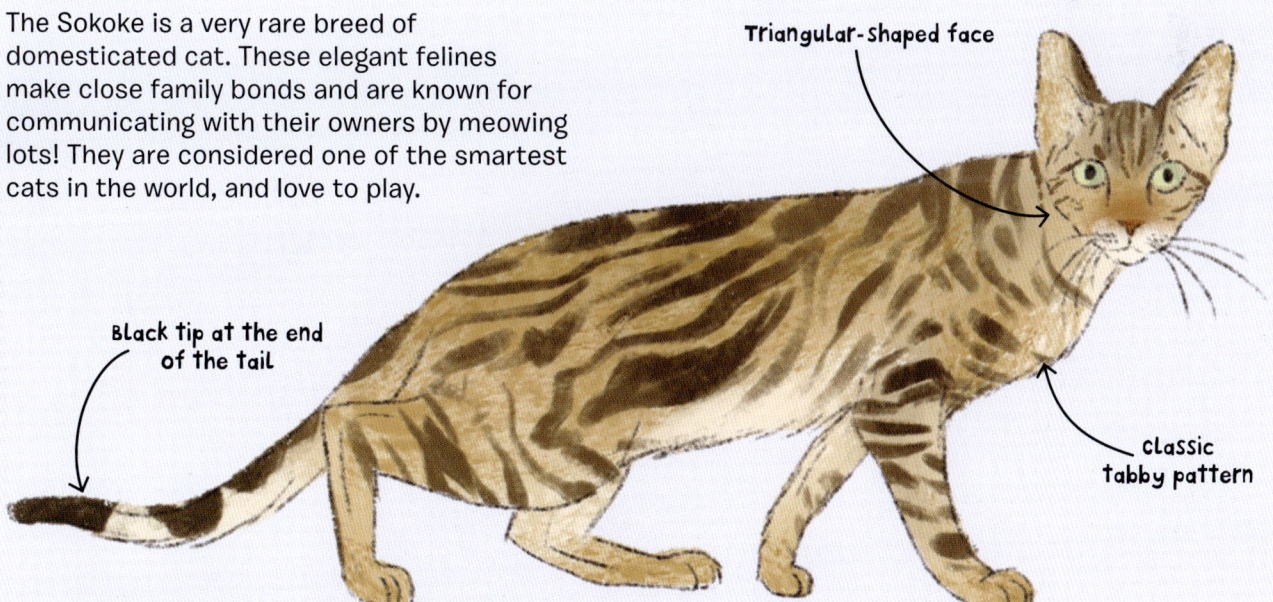

Triangular-shaped face

Black tip at the end of the tail

classic tabby pattern

**ORIGIN:** Kenya
**COAT:** Coarse and glossy
**PERSONALITY:** Friendly and curious

GROOMING
AFFECTION
PLAYFULNESS

# COOL SHORT-HAIRED CATS

## Exotic Shorthair

This cat has a very expressive face, and spends most of the time looking very grumpy! The exotic shorthair can be very affectionate and loyal toward its owners, but not so much strangers. It likes playing but enjoys cuddles on the sofa just as much!

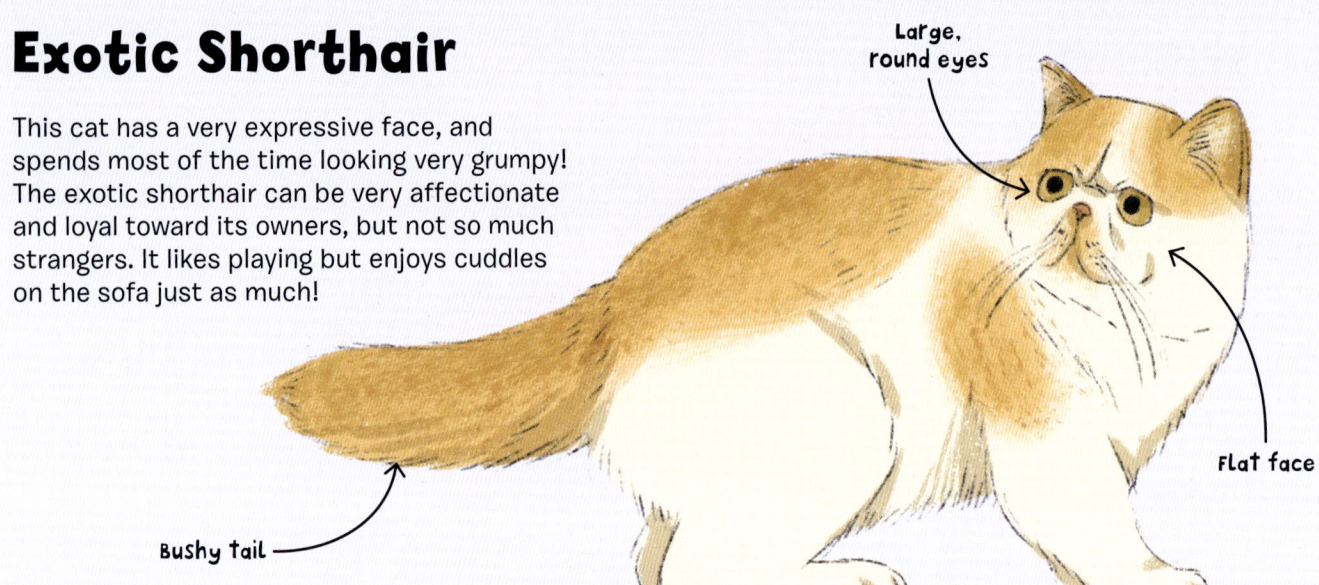

Large, round eyes

Flat face

Bushy tail

| | |
|---|---|
| **ORIGIN:** USA | **GROOMING** 🐾🐾🐾 |
| **COAT:** Soft and thick | **AFFECTION** 🐾🐾🐾 |
| **PERSONALITY:** Friendly and calm | **PLAYFULNESS** 🐾🐾🐾 |

## Oriental

The Oriental is a breed of domestic cat that has been developed from the Siamese cat. Their coats range from the brightest white to the darkest black. They are known for having large, wide-stretching ears! This slender feline enjoys being around its owners and has lots of energy for them too.

Triangular, long shaped head

Almond-shaped eyes

Long, thin neck

Keeps its owners busy and on their toes!

| | |
|---|---|
| **ORIGIN:** United Kingdom | **GROOMING** 🐾 |
| **COAT:** Thin and glossy | **AFFECTION** 🐾🐾🐾🐾🐾 |
| **PERSONALITY:** Lively and intelligent | **PLAYFULNESS** 🐾🐾🐾🐾 |

**STAND OUT FROM THE CROWD**

# Seychellois

Seychellois are elegant and slender cats. Similarly to Oriental cats (page 18), they are known for their large, wide ears and long triangular faces. These active cats are very vocal and want their owners' attention at all times!

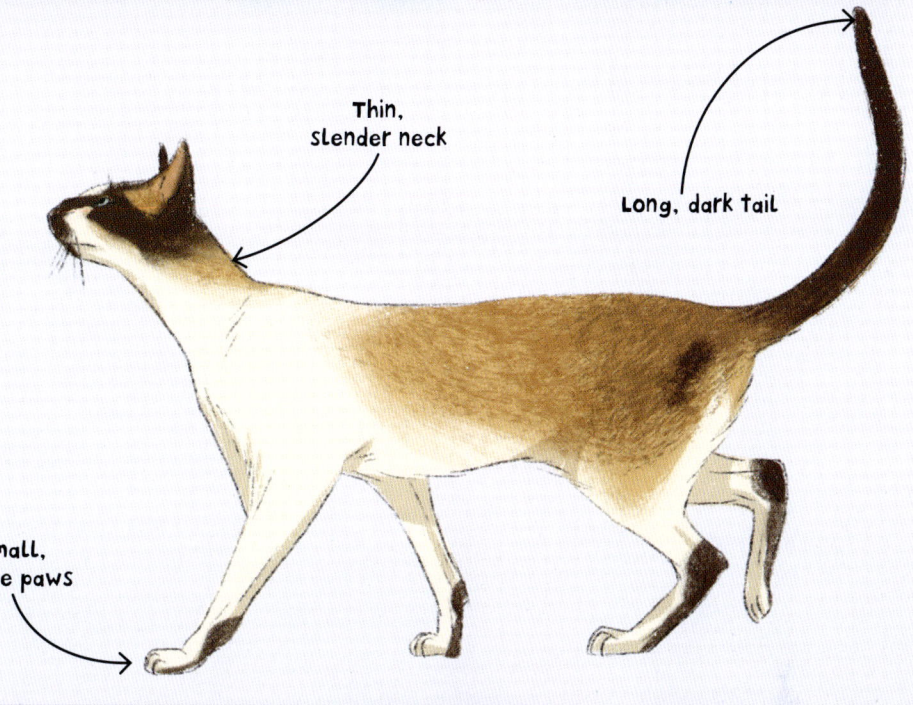

- Thin, slender neck
- Long, dark tail
- Small, white paws

**ORIGIN:** United Kingdom
**COAT:** Short and glossy
**PERSONALITY:** Loving and sociable

| | | | | | |
|---|---|---|---|---|---|
| GROOMING | 🐾 | 🐾 | · | · | · |
| AFFECTION | 🐾 | 🐾 | 🐾 | 🐾 | 🐾 |
| PLAYFULNESS | 🐾 | 🐾 | 🐾 | 🐾 | 🐾 |

# Suffolk

This striking cat is often described as having dog-like characteristics. They prefer being in the company of their owner, rather than going out to explore! The Suffolk comes in two different shades: chocolate brown and lilac.

- Bright, green eyes!
- Strong, muscular body
- Long, sturdy legs

**ORIGIN:** United Kingdom
**COAT:** Short and thin
**PERSONALITY:** Loyal and friendly

| | | | | | |
|---|---|---|---|---|---|
| GROOMING | 🐾 | 🐾 | · | · | · |
| AFFECTION | 🐾 | 🐾 | 🐾 | 🐾 | 🐾 |
| PLAYFULNESS | 🐾 | 🐾 | 🐾 | 🐾 | · |

# COOL SHORT-HAIRED CATS

## American Shorthair

Despite its name, the American shorthair descended from working cats from Europe. They were taken over to the USA in the 1600s, after being used on boats to protect cargo from **rodents**. Now popular pets, these cats are playful, curious, and still love to hunt!

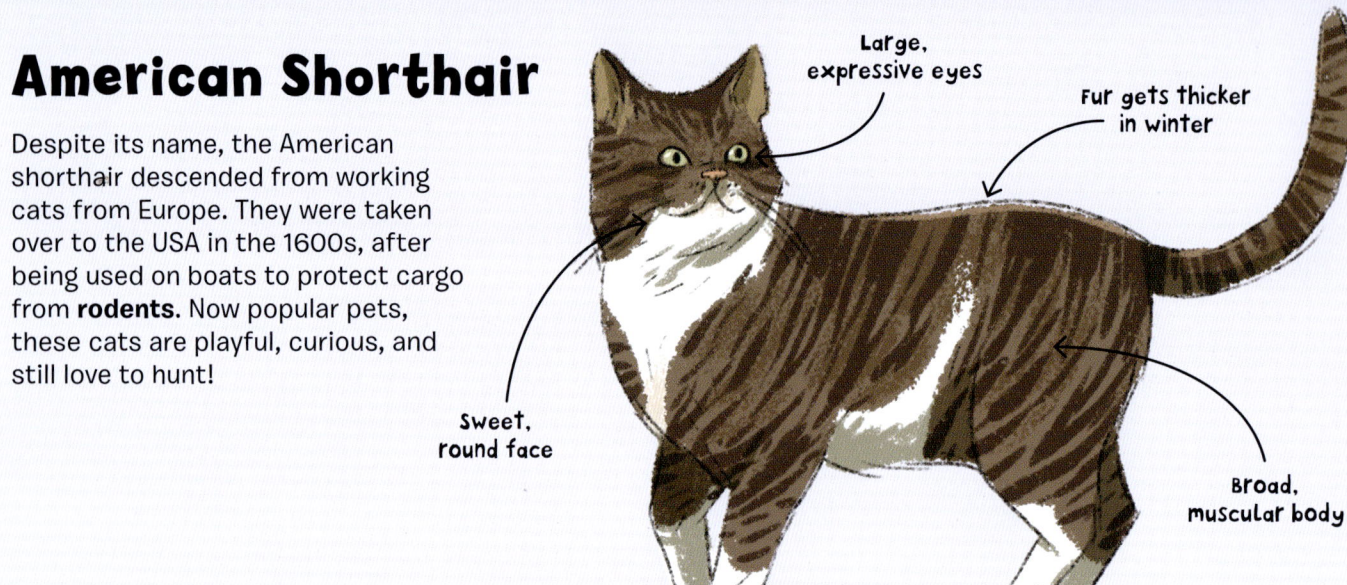

- Large, expressive eyes
- Fur gets thicker in winter
- Sweet, round face
- Broad, muscular body

**ORIGIN:** USA
**COAT:** Short and thick
**PERSONALITY:** Independent and curious

GROOMING 🐾🐾
AFFECTION 🐾🐾🐾
PLAYFULNESS 🐾🐾🐾🐾

- Enjoys hunting
- Short, pointed ears

AROUND THE WORLD 21

# British Shorthair

This cute companion is one of the oldest breeds in the United Kingdom. Although sometimes called British Blues after their lovely silver-blue coat, they can also be cream or tabby. Calm and well-behaved, they make perfect pets.

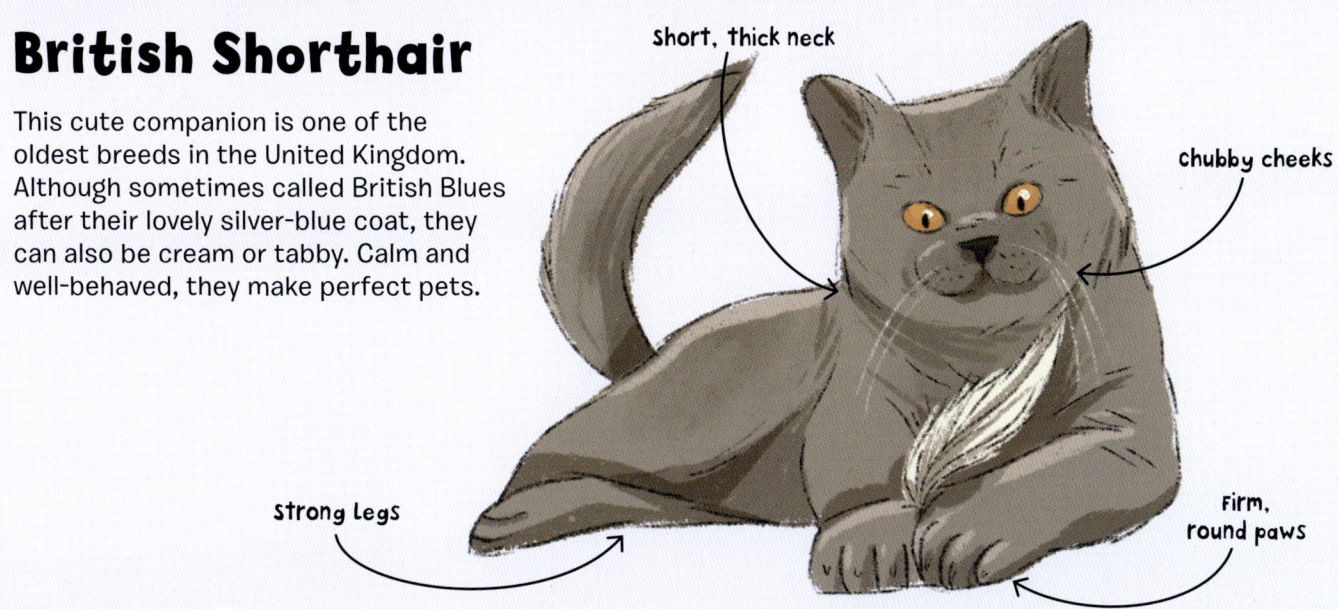

**ORIGIN:** United Kingdom
**COAT:** Short and thick
**PERSONALITY:** Loyal and laid-back

GROOMING 🐾🐾🐾🐾🐾
AFFECTION 🐾🐾🐾🐾🐾
PLAYFULNESS 🐾🐾🐾🐾🐾

# Chinese Li Hua

Also known as Dragon Li, this breed is thought to have descended from wildcats centuries ago! Considered one of the earliest domestic cats, this fine feline is good with families and pets, and is easy to care for.

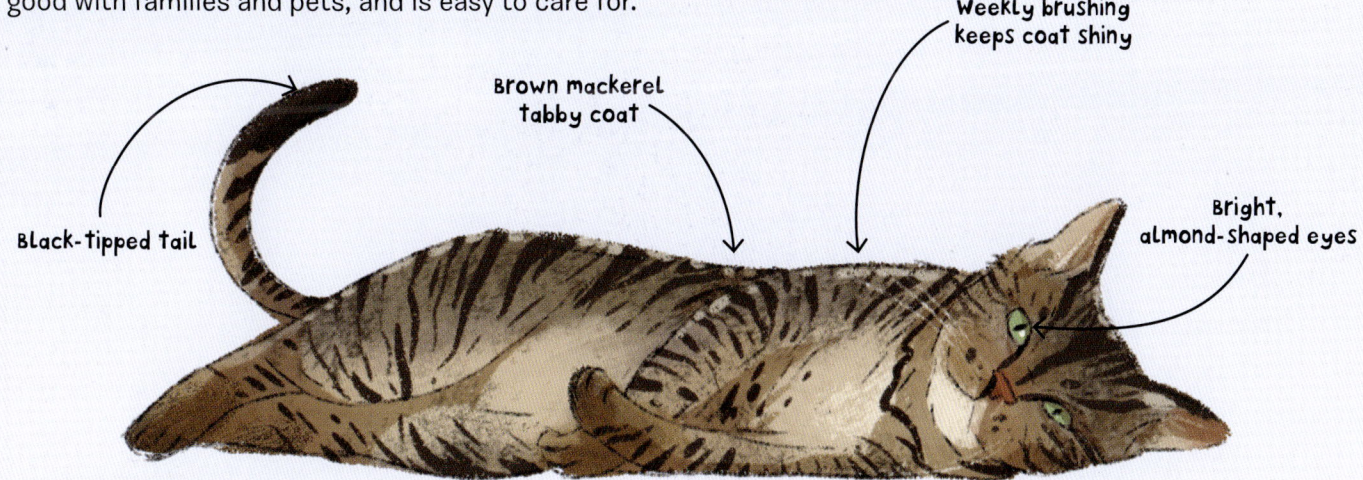

**ORIGIN:** China
**COAT:** Short and smooth
**PERSONALITY:** Intelligent and friendly

GROOMING 🐾🐾🐾🐾🐾
AFFECTION 🐾🐾🐾🐾🐾
PLAYFULNESS 🐾🐾🐾🐾🐾

# COOL CAT FACTS

What else is there to know about the amazing world of short-haired cats? Let's uncover more intriguing facts about these fluffy felines.

## RIGHT OR LEFT?

Just as humans are right-handed or left-handed, cats are right-pawed and left-pawed! It's believed that most female cats will put their right foot forward first, whereas male cats will choose their left foot to lean on first.

This cat is most likely a male because it's putting its left foot first.

## SO MANY SOUNDS!

Cats are able to make up to 100 different sounds! This is an impressive amount compared to dogs, who can only make 10 sounds. These sounds include meows, purrs, hisses, growls, and many more.

Hissing

Meowing

Growling

# BIG BRAINS

A cat's brain is very similar to a human's brain! It's around 90% similar in shape and size. Cats are really smart, too. They can tell how we're feeling, and understand if we're happy or sad.

# MUSICAL MEOWING

Cats are known for their pleasing purrs and meows. Scientists discovered that, since cats have been domesticated, the sounds they make have become nicer for humans to hear.

It's believed that cats don't meow at anything other than humans!

# CAT COMMUNICATION

Because cats can't talk like humans do, it's important for us to understand how cats communicate instead. Let's explore some of the unique ways that cats show how they are feeling.

## BODY LANGUAGE

Cats will often use their ears, eyes, whiskers, and tail to communicate how they are feeling.

If a cat's ears are pointing forwards, it usually means they are interested and alert to their surroundings.

The eyes of a cat will get larger when they are dealing with big emotions, like excitement or worry.

When a cat feels threatened, they will often move their whiskers to face towards whatever they are feeling threatened by.

A cat's tail has a language of its own! Cats will often use their tails to show how they are feeling. For example, if their tail is straight up, a cat may be happy, but if they are held low to the ground, they may be sad or frightened.

## POSTURE

You can tell if a cat is happy to be approached by their **posture**. If a cat is lying down in a relaxed way or walking towards you, that means it is feeling friendly. If a cat is rolling around from side to side, this means they are feeling playful! However, if a cat has its back arched and fur standing up, watch out! This means it is getting ready to pounce!

Friendly cat wanting attention

Cat getting ready to pounce

Playful cat rolling around

## SMELL

Cats have an excellent sense of smell. When they are exploring outdoors, cats will often mark their **territory** with pee so other cats know to stay away.

## TOUCH

Cats also communicate by rubbing their bodies on surfaces, and even other cats! This helps them to make other feline friends, as well as mark those cats as part of their group.

Cats will also rub and lick their owners to include them as part of their feline family!

# NAME THAT CAT

Can you work out which cat each of these pictures are a part of? Clues have been provided for you based on facts in this book.

CLUE: These cats are described as having dog-like characteristics.

CLUE: These cats have white paws which gives them their name.

CLUE: These cats are thought to be one of the earliest domestic felines. They are also known as the Dragon Li.

CLUE: These cats look like a small version of a tiger.

CLUE: These wild-looking cats are believed to have descended from Ethiopia.

CLUE: These cats have very expressive faces, and spend most of their time looking grumpy.

CLUE: These cats have been developed from the Siamese cat. They have triangular, long shaped heads.

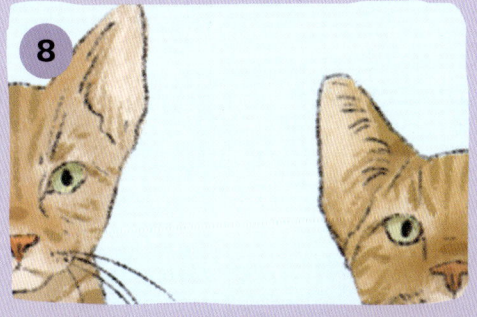

CLUE: These cats have the same spotted tabby coat and distinctive eyes as an ocelot.

CLUE: These cats have a soft, shadowy appearance which gives them their misty name.

CLUE: These cats are considered a good luck charm in Thailand.

Answers can be found on page 32.

# WHAT'S THAT CAT?

Now that you have read all about these cool cats, how good are you at identifying them? There are 20 different cats to figure out. Use the information in the book to help you.

**What am I?**
A. Chinese Li Hua
B. Bombay
C. Seychellois

**What am I?**
A. Suffolk
B. British Shorthair
C. Ocicat

**What am I?**
A. Sokoke
B. Oriental
C. Snowshoe

**What am I?**
A. Burmese
B. Oriental
C. Bombay

**What am I?**
A. Korat
B. Toyger
C. Seychellois

**What am I?**
A. Australian Mist
B. Havana
C. Abyssinian

**What am I?**
A. Korat
B. Chinese Li Hua
C. Savannah

**What am I?**
A. Bengal
B. Havana
C. British Shorthair

**What am I?**
A. Ocicat
B. Australian Mist
C. American Shorthair

**What am I?**
A. Suffolk
B. American Shorthair
C. Chartreux

Answers can be found on page 32.

**What am I?**
A. Ocicat
B. Burmese
C. Toyger

**What am I?**
A. Toyger
B. Abyssinian
C. Chartreux

**What am I?**
A. Savannah
B. Abyssinian
C. American Shorthair

**What am I?**
A. Savannah
B. Korat
C. Bengal

**What am I?**
A. British Shorthair
B. Sokoke
C. Snowshoe

**What am I?**
A. Havana
B. Seychellois
C. Snowshoe

**What am I?**
A. Oriental
B. Exotic Shorthair
C. Chinese Li Hua

**What am I?**
A. Snowshoe
B. Exotic Shorthair
C. Suffolk

**What am I?**
A. Burmese
B. Bengal
C. Sokoke

**What am I?**
A. Australian Mist
B. Suffolk
C. Bombay

# GLOSSARY

**Ear wax** – a substance made by ears that helps keep them clean and protected from dust and dirt.

**Descendants** – people or animals that are related to an individual or group who lived in the past. For example, you are a descendant of your parents and grandparents.

**Domestic** – an animal that has been tamed or trained to live or work with humans.

**Matting** – when an animal's fur gets tangled and stuck together, usually because it hasn't been brushed or groomed.

**Mucus** - a slimy substance made by our bodies to help trap dirt and germs.

**Posture** - the way an animal or human holds their body when they're sitting, standing, or moving around.

**Rehoming shelters** - places where cats (or other animals) who were lost, stray or given up by their owners are looked after until they can be adopted into a new home.

**Rodents** - small mammals with sharp front teeth, such as mice or squirrels.

**Slender** - something that is thin and narrow.

**Territory** - a specific area that belongs to someone or something.

**Unique** - something that stands out and is completely different from everything else.

# INDEX

**A**
Abyssinian 11, 17, 28-29, 32
American shorthair 20, 28-29, 32
Australian mist 17, 28-29, 32

**B**
bathing 6
Bengal 15, 28-29, 32
Bombay 13, 28-29, 32
British shorthair 21, 28-29, 32
Burmese 11, 17, 28-29, 32

**C**
Chartreux 13, 28-29, 32
Chinese Li Hua 21, 28-29, 32
cleaning 6-7
communication 17, 22-23, 24-25

**E**
Exotic shorthair 18, 29, 32

**F**
features 8-9
    ears 7, 8-9, 11, 13, 14-15, 17, 18-19, 20, 24
    paws 7, 8-9, 15, 16, 19, 21, 22, 26
    senses 8-9, 25
    teeth 7, 8-9, 30

**G**
grooming 5, 6, 9, 10

**H**
Havana 4, 12, 28-29, 32

**K**
Korat 12, 28-29, 32

**O**
Ocicat 15, 28-29, 32
Oriental 18-19, 28-29, 32

**S**
Savannah 14, 28-29, 32
Seychellois 19, 28-29, 32
Snowshoe 4, 16, 28-29, 32
Sokoke 17, 28-29, 32
species 4-5, 10
Suffolk 19, 28-29, 32

**T**
Toyger 14, 28-29, 32

## NAME THAT CAT ANSWERS

1 - Suffolk
2 - Snowshoe
3 - Chinese Li Hua
4 - Toyger
5 - Abyssinian
6 - Oriental
7 - Exotic Shorthair
8 - Ocicat
9 - Australian Mist
10 - Korat

## WHAT'S THAT CAT ANSWERS

1 - A. Chinese Li Hua
2 - B. British Shorthair
3 - B. Oriental
4 - C. Bombay
5 - C. Seychellois
6 - B. Havana
7 - A. Korat
8 - A. Bengal
9 - A. Ocicat
10 - C. Chartreux
11 - C. Toyger
12 - B. Abyssinian
13 - C. American Shorthair
14 - A. Savannah
15 - B. Sokoke
16 - C. Snowshoe
17 - B. Exotic Shorthair
18 - C. Suffolk
19 - A. Burmese
20 - A. Australian Mist

Picture Credits:
(abbreviations: t=top, b=bottom, m=middle, l=left, r=right)

Shutterstock: AJR_photo 29tr; Akifyeva S 29mr; Aleks Silchenko 25br; Alena Ozerova 22tl; BBbirdZ 6br; Bez_bretelky 28bl; COULANGES 29ml; Darya Lavinskaya 29tl; Dasha Parfenova 29bl; DavidTB 9tl; Elenavolf 7bl; Fantom_rd 24bl; Gino Santa Maria 28mr; HelloRF Zcool 29tr; Ivanonva Ksenia 25tl; Jilin Su 28tl; John Danow 24tl; Katamount 25tm; Katniss studio 28br; Kutikova Ekaterina 29tl; Leo Prez 29br; Maliflower73 9bl; MC Jaarsveld 25tr; Mny_Jhee 24mr; Nils Jacobi 9br; Pokofoto 22bm; Raul Photography 7tr; RealPeopleStudio 6tl; Seregraff 28ml; Sirtravelalot 7tl; Skymar27 28mr; Slowmotiongli 28ml; Surachet Jo 9tr; Suraram Kag 25bl; Svetlana Rey 7br; Svyatoslav Balan 29mr; Truenos86 28tl; Viktor Sergeevich 28tr; Vivver 28tr; Wavebreakmedia 23tl; Yhelfman 22bl; Yuliya Alekseeva 29ml; Zhuravlev Andrey 22br.

Every effort has been made to trace the copyright holders, and we apologise in advance for any unintentional omissions. We would be pleased to insert the appropriate acknowledgements in any subsequent edition of this publication.

## ABOUT THE AUTHOR

Eliza Jeffery is a children's book author based in Falmouth. She is passionate about helping children explore and enjoy the big world around them. She loves exploring Cornwall, and can often be found reading a book and eating a bowl of mussels by the sea!

## ABOUT THE ILLUSTRATOR

Marina Halak is a talented illustrator of children's books from Ukraine. Her stunning illustrations are inspired by her own childhood, children, nature, magical moments and fairy tales. Marina is also the illustrator behind the series, *Dogs*.